"A Traveler's Passport to Etiquette in a Post-Pandemic World"

By

Online Etiquette Expert

Lisa Mirza Grotts

Dedication

For JJM. Your love was the greatest adventure of all!

Foreword

Lisa Mirza Grotts' *A Traveler's Passport to Etiquette in a Post-Pandemic World* is an essential guide, offering crucial insights on how to gracefully navigate the world's evolving cultural norms and etiquette.

-Christopher Elliott is a nationally syndicated columnist: Forbes and USA Today

Lisa Mirza Grotts

A journey is like a marriage. The certain way
to be wrong is to think you can control it."

~ John Steinbeck ~

Table of Contents

Lisa Mirza Grotts

Preface

Air Travel 2.0: Navigating The New Normal

Turbulence Behind Us: Cleared for Take-Off

The Pandemic of 2020 illuminated our greatest strengths: unity, compassion, and resilience. Through collective effort and empathy, we faced challenges head-on and emerged stronger, more connected, and with a renewed appreciation for life's simple joys. As we navigate the ever-evolving landscape of air travel, we find ourselves in a world where marijuana is legal, yet we may encounter 'mask shaming' if we opt not to wear one. The handshake, once a common gesture, is now viewed with caution. The national pastime of "don't stand so close" continues to shape our daily interactions.

The Jet Reset: Plane and Simple

Travel is more than just a change of scenery—it's a profound opportunity to explore, learn, and grow. It provides a unique chance to immerse ourselves in diverse cultures, embrace local traditions, and adapt our behaviors to resonate with the communities we encounter. My revised book, *A Traveler's Passport to Etiquette in a Post-Pandemic World*, is designed to guide you through every phase of an airplane journey—from pre-flight etiquette and suitcase strategies to terminal thrills, boarding bliss, cabin comfort, and smart travel tips. The Pandemic of 2020 introduced new safety protocols that have now become standard practice. Mask-wearing at 30,000 feet, social distancing, and enhanced hygiene measures are now essential aspects of the travel experience. Navigating these realities has added a new layer to travel etiquette, underscoring the importance of patience, flexibility, and empathy. So, pack your sense of adventure along with your etiquette, and let's embark on a journey where each destination offers valuable lessons in discovery, direction, and diplomacy.

Chapter 1:
The New Rules of Air Travel Post Pandemic

Fasten Your Seatbelt: Air Travel in a Changed World

The pandemic has fundamentally transformed air travel, introducing a range of new rules and protocols designed to prioritize health and safety while improving the overall travel experience. Passengers now navigate an environment marked by heightened hygiene standards, including comprehensive cleaning procedures and mask mandates in many regions. Social distancing practices and contactless technologies—such as mobile boarding passes and self-check-in kiosks—have become standard to minimize physical interactions. Travelers are also encouraged to stay informed about evolving travel restrictions such as vaccination and testing mandates, which can vary by destination and change frequently.

These new protocols represent a significant shift towards a more health-conscious approach to air travel, designed to ensure a safer journey in a constantly evolving global landscape. In a world irrevocably transformed by COVID-19, air travel has undergone a profound metamorphosis. What was once a routine experience now involves navigating new rules. From the evolving safety measures to the adjustment of shifting social expectations, the journey has increasingly become about cultivating patience and adaptability, just as much as it is about reaching your intended destination.

As we adjust to these changes, it's essential to grasp the new rules of air travel and how they impact our flying experience. Buckle up and prepare for a closer look at how air travel has evolved in this transformed world.

A Traveler's Passport to Etiquette in a Post-Pandemic World

Significant Changes in Air Travel Since 2020

- **Air Filtration Systems**. HEPA filters have become more prominent to filter out airborne particles, including viruses.

- **Contactless Technology**. There has been a significant shift toward contactless check-ins, boarding procedures, and in-flight services. Mobile boarding passes and digital payment systems are the norm.

- **Enhanced Cleaning and Sanitization**. Airlines have adopted more stringent cleaning protocols, incorporating disinfectant sprays, conducting regular cleanings of high-touch surfaces, and offering hand sanitizer onboard.

- **Essential Gear**. Masks have become a crucial travel companion. Pack extra to ensure you're always prepared.

- **Flexible Booking Policies**. Airlines have implemented more flexible booking and cancellation policies to better accommodate the uncertainty that travelers often encounter. In many cases, this includes allowing changes without fees or providing travel credits for canceled flights.

- **Mask Mandates and Health Protocols**. Although mask mandates have relaxed, some airlines still require masks, particularly during outbreaks. Check the latest guidelines before you travel.

- **Modified In-Flight Services**. Many airlines have scaled back or adjusted in-flight meal services to minimize contact between passengers and crew. Pre-packaged meals and snacks are the norm.

- **On-Board Entertainment**. For a touchless experience, bring your own devices for movies and music instead of those provided by the airline.

- **Patience**. Traveling post-COVID requires an extra dose of patience. Never leave home without it.

- **Preparation**. Equip your carry-on with a COVID cleaning kit: wipes, masks, and gloves to maintain a clean and safe environment.

- **Respect Boundaries**. Maintain social distance and avoid judging others. Address any issues with the cabin crew to avoid conflicts with passengers.

- **Seat Assignments**. Social distancing protocols might lead to unexpected seat changes or even upgrades, such as a checkerboard seating arrangement. Go with the flow.

- **Social Distancing Measures**. Initially, airlines blocked middle seats to encourage social distancing. Though most have since reverted to full capacity, many carriers have revised their boarding and deplaning procedures to minimize crowding and enhance passenger safety during these processes.

- **Travel Restrictions**. Quarantine requirements and travel bans are in place and implemented by various countries and evolving on a global level. Know before you go!

- **Emergency Protocols**. Familiarize yourself with emergency protocols while traveling. Notify the crew if you show symptoms of illness.

- **Travel Insurance**. Consider purchasing travel insurance that covers COVID-related disruptions or health issues.

- **Digital Tools and Apps**. Use apps for travel updates, health information, and navigation to enhance your travel experience.

- **Cultural Sensitivity**. Be aware of varying health and safety norms in different countries and adapt accordingly.

- **Customer Service**. Handle disruptions, such as delays or cancellations, by communicating with airline staff and seeking assistance as needed.

- **Preparation for Unforeseen Changes**. Stay flexible and check for last-minute updates or changes to travel regulations.

Chapter 2:
Adventure Prep: Planning, Prepping, Packing

Mapping out your Adventure. Planning your trip is your gateway to peace of mind, ensuring that every aspect is carefully considered. The adventure starts well before you leave home, and the secret to a smooth journey lies in meticulous preparation. Begin by creating a flexible yet detailed itinerary, outlining key activities and must-visit spots. Customize your packing list based on the climate and the specifics of your trip, prioritizing essentials that boost comfort and convenience—such as versatile outfits, necessary toiletries, and compact travel gadgets. But preparation doesn't stop at packing: immerse yourself in the culture of your destination by researching local customs and traditions. Double-check your itinerary. Confirm all accommodations, and ensure your travel documents are up-to-date to travel with confidence to avoid unnecessary stress. A successful vacation plan boils down to simplicity: review your schedule, verify your bookings, and pack strategically. Keep vital items like medications, jewelry, and important documents within reach. With everything well-organized, you'll be ready to dive into your vacation with enthusiasm and ease.

Securing an Ideal Seat. Mirror, Mirror on the Wall, 9B is the seat for me! In today's world of creative airline fees, selecting your seat during booking isn't just a preference—it's essential. Whether you favor the aisle for more legroom or the window for the view, securing your seat in advance prevents unwelcome surprises and keeps you near your travel companions. For the tech-savvy traveler, seat selection apps are invaluable. These apps provide detailed information about plane layouts, including seat recline and proximity to restrooms, helping you choose the best spot. Opting to skip seat selection might seem trivial, but it can land you in the dreaded middle seat. While the temptation of an upgrade is always there, remember that it's often a gamble. By the time you reach the airport, premium seats may be long gone, leaving you in a less-than-ideal spot. The most reliable way to guarantee your preferred seat is to become a loyal flyer. Earning elite status ensures you'll consistently enjoy a comfortable seat every time you board, so you can skip the turn right into coach class.

From A to Z: The Essentials

- **Alarm Company**. Notify your alarm company about your trip and provide emergency contact details.

- **Allergy Considerations**. If allergic to service animals, notify the airline to arrange suitable seating.

- **Allow Time for Crowds**. Be prepared for long lines and delays. Plan to arrive early for the check-in process.

- **Air Tags**. These tracking devices help locate lost items.

- **Avoid Overpacking**. Pack only the essentials to leave room for new purchases. Bring one nice outfit for formal events, along with versatile shoes.

- **Avoid Standing Out**. Leave valuables and designer luggage at home to maintain discretion and ensure safety.

- **Check Airline Requirements**. Verify checked luggage weight and size limits with your airline, as many have reduced their allowances.

- **Color Coordinate**. Choose three versatile colors (e.g., blue, black, white) for easy mixing and matching of outfits.

- **Credit Card Notification**. Inform your credit card companies of your travel dates and destinations to prevent holds on your cards.

- **Dress Code**. Respect local dress norms and customs to blend in and show cultural sensitivity.

- **Dress Comfortably**. Layer your clothing to adapt to varying cabin temperatures, but avoid overly casual attire such as sweatpants.

- **E-Identification**. Take a screenshot of all forms of ID and keep in a separate file.

- **Bulkheads**. Request seats in exit rows or bulkheads for extra legroom, but be aware that they may not recline.

A Traveler's Passport to Etiquette in a Post-Pandemic World

- **Extra Baggage**. Bring an extra duffel bag for shopping or to reinforce your suitcase.

- **Flight Confirmation**. Verify your flight and seat assignment 24 hours before departure, and again on the day of your flight.

- **Foreign Currency**. Obtain a small amount of foreign currency before traveling abroad.

- **Fragrances**. Avoid wearing perfume and aftershaves to prevent discomfort for others.

- **Frequent Flyer Perks**. Enroll in frequent flyer programs to earn rewards and gain access to better seating options.

- **Gratuity**. Understand tipping practices in different countries, as many include gratuity in the dining bill.

- **Handbag Hacks**. Carry heavy or bulky items in your handbag or backpack so you won't be charged in checked luggage.

- **Health Guidelines**. Stay informed about health protocols to ensure safety and comfort.

- **Itinerary**. Leave an itinerary with family members that includes flight details, hotel information, and emergency contacts.

- **Keys**. Keep house and car keys with you until you reach your destination.

- **Learn Basic Phrases**. Familiarize yourself with essential phrases like "hello," "goodbye," and "how do I get to the airport?" in the local language.

- **Leverage Your Status**. If you lack status, consider purchasing a day pass for access to airport lounges for a more comfortable experience.

- **Luggage Rules**. Review your airline's luggage size, contents, and carry-on policies in advance.

- **Luggage Tags**. Ensure your luggage has tags with your name, and phone number on the outside and inside of your bags.

- **Mail and Newspaper**. Arrange for mail and newspaper delivery to be stopped while you're away.

- **Online Tools**. Check online apps for plane configurations to avoid seats that don't recline.

- **Pack Light**. Travel with minimal baggage to leave room for souvenirs and to avoid excess fees.

- **Permitted Items**. Know which items are allowed and prohibited. For regular updates, visit TSA Travel Tips.

- **Plastic Bag Backup**. Pack plastic bags to protect against spills.

- **Respect Local Politics**. Keep political opinions to yourself and respect the local political climate.

- **Seat Selection**. Select your seat when booking to sit with family or friends to secure your preferred spot.

- **Shoes as Storage**. Utilize your shoes to store linear items such as tampons, hairspray, or brushes.

- **Tipping**. Carry small bills for tipping porters, typically $5. Some airlines may charge this as a fee instead of a gratuity.

- **Valuables**. Carry valuables such as cash, medicines, and jewelry in your hand luggage.

- **Voicemail**. Do not change your voicemail greeting to indicate you're away.

- **Wear and Discard**. Pack items that are nearing the end of their use so you can discard them and save space for new purchases.

- **Wrapped Gifts**. Never carry wrapped gifts through security. Instead, mail them in advance.

Pre-Departure Checklist:

- Bathrobes, pajamas, slippers

- Beach towels, swimsuits

- Belts, socks

A Traveler's Passport to Etiquette in a Post-Pandemic World

- Bras, underwear
- Coats, sweaters
- Dress shoes
- Hats, scarves
- Shirts, pants
- Shorts, t-shirts
- Suits, dresses
- Ties, cufflinks
- Walking shoes
- Workout attire and shoes

Toiletries:

- Band-aids, nasal spray
- Brush, comb
- Contact lenses
- Deodorant
- Hair products and accessories
- Hygiene products
- Liquid: Adhere to TSA 3-1-1 rules (3-ounce bottles)

"Good company in a journey makes the way seem shorter."

~ Izaak Walton ~

Chapter 3:
The Airport Experience: Terminal Thrills

Ready. Set. Jet. Arriving at the airport doesn't have to be just a step toward your flight—it can be an enjoyable part of your journey. Start by embracing the airport's amenities, such as comfortable lounges, diverse dining options, and unique shopping experiences. Take a leisurely walk through the terminal, explore art installations, or enjoy a meal at a gourmet restaurant. You could also use the time to relax in a quiet lounge or catch up on a book or work. Many airports offer facilities to enhance comfort, like spa services, sleep pods, and children's play areas. By focusing on these opportunities for relaxation and enjoyment, you can make the pre-flight phase a pleasant and stress-free start to your trip.

Sky Lounge Tips: Where Comfort Meets Convenience

- **Arrive Early**. Take advantage of amenities such as espresso, newspapers, or a relaxing massage.

- **Be Considerate of Space**. Avoid taking up more room than necessary, especially during busy times. Be mindful of your carry-on.

- **Clean Up After Yourself**. Leave your area tidy, as if your mother weren't there to clean up.

- **Keep Your Luggage Out of the Way**. Position your bags in a corner, by a window, or between your legs to prevent hazards.

- **Scout Out Your Ideal Spot**. Do a quick walkthrough to find the best seat.

- **Share Power Outlets**. Be courteous and share access of electrical outlets with other travelers.

- **Stay Aware of the Time**. Be mindful of your flight schedule, as gate announcements are becoming less common.

- **Use a Quiet Voice**. Remember, lounges are shared spaces, so keep conversations to a low volume.

- **Use Headphones for Calls and Entertainment**. When making calls or enjoying media, wear headphones to maintain a peaceful environment.

The Airport Staycation: Finding Rest Amid Delays

While an airport sleepover is far from ideal, when travel plans go awry, it's essential to explore alternatives beyond the usual options. No one expects to spend the night at an airport unless they're catching a red-eye flight, and even then, the amenities fall short of home comforts. If you're faced with unexpected downtime, look for quiet zones, sleeping pods, or airport lounges. These spaces often provide necessities like restrooms, showers, snacks, drinks, Wi-Fi, and semi-private, comfortable seating. Some airports even offer cots for stranded travelers. However, if you're stuck with basic airport seating, here are four etiquette tips to make your experience more bearable:

1. **Be Considerate**. An airport is not your home. Use headphones for entertainment, and keep phone conversations private. If you tend to snore, be ready for an early wake up call.

2. **Be Prepared and Courteous**. Take responsibility for your belongings and trash. Leave the space better than you found it.

3. **Keep It Clean**. Just as you'd freshen up after a long flight, do the same after a long night at the airport.

4. **Stock Up**. Many airports close overnight, so be sure to visit a convenience store to stock up on essentials and snacks. It may be a while before your next meal.

Queue Culture: 4 Ways to Navigate Line Etiquette

1. **Cutting in Line**. Cutting the line is generally unacceptable. However, in urgent situations like tight connections or family emergencies, you can politely ask those around you or seek

assistance from an airline attendant. It's important to be assertive, not aggressive, to avoid conflict.

2. **Handling Line Cutters**. If someone cuts in line, it's best to avoid confrontation, which can escalate to aggressive behavior.

3. **Holding a Place**. It's acceptable to ask someone to hold your place if you need to use the restroom or grab food, especially if you have small children. However, always be considerate and understand if others are unable to agree.

4. **Switching Lines**. Switching lines is acceptable if done courteously and without disruption.

Gate Expectations: 11 Tips to Navigate Terminal Etiquette

1. **Be Mindful of Unsupervised Children**. Consideration for others is key to a smooth travel experience.

2. **Boarding and Deplaning**. Don't crowd the gate. Wait until your row is called before boarding to avoid unnecessary congestion. Follow the same protocol when deplaning: if you're in row 28, wait for row 27 to exit first.

3. **Check-in Early**. Skip long lines and avoid the hassle of bulky luggage and flight anxiety.

4. **Don't Be a Gate Rusher**. Wait your turn and let those who need to board first without blocking their way.

5. **Don't Be the Person Holding Up Security**. Prepare your liquids, belt, shoes, and jacket in advance. Keep your ticket and identification ready to avoid delaying other passengers and be prepared to show your ID multiple times until you board.

6. **Don't Crowd the Luggage Carousel**. Give everyone space and avoid being pushy.

7. **Don't Watch Movies Without Headphones**. Respect others' space and keep the noise to yourself.

8. **Follow Pilot Instructions**. Follow the pilot's instructions, particularly about seating before takeoff and when the seatbelt sign is on. This ensures your safety and helps prevent delays.

9. **Outlet Hoggers**. There are plenty to go around, so use them like you would gym equipment: think 30 minutes max.

10. **Plane Talk**. Understand the difference between "direct" and "nonstop" flights. A direct flight may include one or more stops but doesn't require you to switch planes. In contrast, a nonstop flight travels to your destination without any stops.

11. **TSA Gatekeepers**. Avoid arguing with airport security and follow their instructions to ensure a smooth process.

"The longest journey is the journey inward."

~ Dag Hammarskjöld ~

Chapter 4:
Soaring Above: On The Plane

Maintaining good manners during your flight is essential for a pleasant experience for everyone on board. Begin by being considerate of your fellow passengers—keep conversations at a moderate volume and use headphones for entertainment to avoid disturbing others. Respect the shared space by reclining your seat gently, checking behind you first; sudden adjustments can disrupt the comfort of those seated behind you. Be mindful of your personal area by keeping your belongings organized and ensuring you don't encroach on your neighbor's space. When using the overhead bins, handle your items with care to prevent accidents. Additionally, practice good hygiene by using the in-flight restrooms considerately. If you require assistance, politely ask the flight attendants rather than making demands. By adhering to these simple yet important guidelines, you help foster a more harmonious and enjoyable flight for everyone.

Who's Who in the Exit Row: 6 Key Players and Rules

1. **Children and Infants.** Passengers under the age of 15 and those traveling with small children or infants are not permitted in exit rows.

2. **Non-English Speakers.** Passengers must be able to understand instructions in English (or the local language used by the airline) and respond to crew commands during an emergency.

3. **Passengers with Size or Mobility Constraints.** Some airlines restrict seating in exit rows for passengers who may not fit comfortably in 'the standard seatbelt, or who have difficulty moving quickly in an emergency.

4. **Passengers Needing Special Assistance.** Those who require a seatbelt extender, have service animals, or need assistance from others should avoid these seats.

5. **Physically Limited Individuals.** Anyone who cannot perform the required emergency functions due to physical limitations is not eligible for an exit row seat.

6. **Those Who Cannot Assist.** If a passenger is unwilling or unable to assist during an emergency, they should not sit in an exit row. This includes those who may be pregnant, hearing impaired, or vision impaired.

Sky's The Limit: 3 Tips for a Smooth Journey

1. **Window Shade Safety Rules.** Keep your window shade raised during takeoff and landing for safety reasons. This practice helps you stay aware of the external environment and assists crew members and first responders during emergencies.

2. **Avoid Going Barefoot in the Restroom.** Keep your feet covered when using the airplane bathroom to minimize exposure to bacteria and maintain hygiene.

3. **Carry-On Bags Within Limits.** Avoid bringing overweight carry-on bags. Stick to the weight limits or consider upgrading to prevent delays and inconveniences.

Sky High Survival: 4 Airplane On-Board Dining Etiquette Tips

1. **Be Patient.** If you need assistance or extra items, wait until the cabin crew is available to help.

2. **Opt for Fragrance-Free Food.** Choose food that is free of strong odors to avoid disturbing fellow passengers.

3. **Minimize Space.** Keep your food and drink area tidy to avoid encroaching on your neighbor's space.

4. **Respect Meal Times.** If your meal is served at a designated time, make an effort to eat it promptly to avoid any delays or complications with the service. Stay patient when food is being cleared, as it may take some time.

Cabin Chronicles: Etiquette in the Sky

Manners don't take a holiday, even at 30,000 feet. Make sure your etiquette is impeccable when you're soaring through the skies. Treat your time on a plane as if you were a guest in someone's living room. This mindset reinforces the importance of consideration and respect. Below are 10 essential Q&As that address common in-flight behaviors:

1. **How to Handle Seat Kicking.** If someone, especially a child, is kicking your seat, kindly address it with their parents. For adults, it's best to let a flight attendant handle the situation.

2. **Are There Any Noise Considerations?** Use headphones for movies and music to avoid disturbing fellow passengers. Airplanes are quiet zones for personal entertainment.

3. **Can You Recline Your Seat?** Yes, you have the right to recline your seat as you've paid for that space. Be mindful of the timing: wait until mealtime is over.

4. **How Do I Deal with Disruptive Passengers?** Do not engage with disruptive or intoxicated passengers; leave the situation to the flight crew to manage safely.

5. **Is It Acceptable to Switch Seats?** If you choose your seat for particular reasons, it's perfectly acceptable to decline a request to switch. However, if the request to switch is mutually beneficial, allowing others to sit together, it's generally considered courteous to accommodate them.

6. **Is It Okay to Bring My Own Food on a Plane?** Bringing your own food is perfectly acceptable, particularly in coach where in-flight meals may be limited. However, it's best to avoid strong-smelling foods to ensure the comfort of fellow passengers in a confined space.

7. **Is It Okay to Remove Shoes or Socks?** While it may be tempting, refrain from walking around the airplane, particularly in the bathroom, without wearing shoes. This practice is both unhygienic and unpleasant for everyone. However, it is acceptable to remove your shoes while seated in your own space.

8. **What If I Have a Pet Allergy?** Airlines are still refining their policies on pets, so it's important to check their regulations. Be mindful of allergies and other passengers when traveling with animals.

9. **What Should Travelers Know About Overhead Bins and Storing Luggage?** Your overhead bin space is located in your class of service. If you're seated in Coach, your luggage should go above your seat, not in First Class. Store your carry-ons neatly, like tacos or library books, to maximize space for other passengers.

10. **Who Gets the Armrest?** The middle seat passenger gets both armrests, as they have the least desirable seat. If you're in a window or aisle seat, be considerate of their limited space. Be mindful of elbow bumping and avoid encroaching on others' space to prevent being labeled a "seat spreader," a less than flattering title.

Dress to Impress: Flight of Fancy

Dressing appropriately for a flight is a vital component of travel etiquette. It's important to uphold a standard of professionalism and respect, even when you're in the air. Recently, there has been a noticeable rise in casual clothing choices, including cutoff shorts, pajamas, and even passengers going barefoot. Different occasions warrant different attire and airplane attire occupies a unique space in between. Here are seven tips to ensure you dress well while traveling:

1. **Avoid Pajamas.** While comfort is key, pajamas are best reserved for bedtime.

2. **Choose Closed-Toe Shoes.** For hygiene reasons, it's best to avoid walking around barefoot or in open-toe sandals.

3. **Dress in Layers.** Plan for varying temperatures by wearing layers that you can adjust as needed.

4. **Keep it Simple.** Stick to practical and neat clothing that won't offend others.

5. **Opt for Comfort and Style.** Choose comfortable yet stylish clothing that reflects respect for yourself and others.

6. **Respect the Space.** Avoid overly revealing or offensive attire that might offend other passengers.

7. **Stay Fresh.** Maintain good personal hygiene to ensure a pleasant environment for everyone on board.

8 Things You Should Avoid Wearing on a Flight:

1. **Flimsy Footwear.** They offer little protection or support.

2. **Heavy Jewelry and Accessories.** They are prone to set off metal detectors at TSA and make a lot of in-flight noise.

3. **High-Heeled Shoes.** They look gorgeous but can impede in an emergency evacuation.

4. **Lace-Up Shoes.** They are cumbersome at security checks and will cause delays.

5. **Pajamas.** They are comfortable but inappropriate in a public setting.

6. **Perfume.** Fragrance can trigger allergies, especially in a confined space.

7. **Revealing or Offensive Attire.** If it makes other people uncomfortable, don't wear it.

8. **Tight Clothing.** Anything that can restrict circulation is never a good idea, especially on transatlantic flights.

The Graceful Exit

As your flight begins its descent, following proper etiquette and safety practices is essential for a seamless transition. Remain seated with your seatbelt securely fastened until the aircraft has come to a complete stop and the seatbelt sign is turned off. When it's time to disembark, adhere to an orderly exit process: passengers seated in the front rows should deplane first, followed by those in the middle rows, and finally, the rear rows. Within each row, exit in the following order: aisle seat first, then the middle seat, and lastly, the window seat.

If you're seated in first class, you will exit before passengers in other cabins. Be attentive to your belongings: retrieve them promptly from the overhead bins to minimize congestion. Keep the aisles and your personal space clear to facilitate a smooth deplaning process. If you have a tight connection and are worried about missing your next flight, politely inform a flight attendant. They can assist by making an announcement to help expedite your exit. Adhering to orderly exit protocol is not merely about following rules; it demonstrates respect and efficiency, ensuring a more pleasant experience for everyone.

"If you don't know where you're going,
any road will lead you there."

~ Lewis Carroll ~

Chapter 5:
Playing It Safe: On The Ground

Arrival and Adjustment: Adapting to New Cultures

Upon arriving at your destination, whether traveling alone or with a group, embracing and adapting to the local culture is essential. By following these tips, you'll find it easier to acclimate to your new surroundings, build meaningful connections, and make a positive impact wherever your journey takes you.

7 Tips on How to Navigate This Transition Effectively

1. **Be Flexible**. Adjust your behavior and expectations to fit the climate. Embracing different social norms and practices will enhance your ability to adapt and enjoy your surroundings.

2. **Communicate Effectively**. If traveling with a group, ensure that everyone is aware of and respects local customs. Clear communication helps prevent misunderstandings and ensures a smoother travel experience for all.

3. **Connect with Locals**. Strive to engage with your surroundings through conversations, guided tours, or participation in local events. Cultivating these connections will provide you with a richer and better understanding of the culture.

4. **Embrace New Experiences**. Embrace your travels with an open mind and a willingness to explore. By adapting to new cultural norms and practices, you will enrich your journey and leave a lasting impression.

5. **Familiarize Yourself with Local Customs**. Before you arrive, research the customs and traditions of your destination. This preparation will help you navigate local practices respectfully and avoid misunderstandings.

6. **Practice Courtesy**. Whether traveling alone or with others, maintain politeness and respect. Showing appreciation for the

locals and being considerate of fellow travelers goes a long way.

7. **Respect Local Traditions**. Follow local etiquette, which encompasses dress codes, social norms, and dining customs. Exhibiting respect not only reflects cultural sensitivity, but also encourages positive interactions.

Stay Safe, Travel Smart: 16 Key Points to Remember

1. **Adapt Your Etiquette**. Recognize that what may seem acceptable to you could be perceived differently by others. Sensitivity to these differences helps avoid misunderstandings.

2. **Be Considerate**. Always cover your sneezes and coughs with a hand or mask to maintain a respectful environment for everyone.

3. **Cash Is No Longer King**. Avoid using cash in public to reduce the risk of theft. Opt for credit/debit cards or mobile payments.

4. **Dress Modestly**. Respect local dress codes and avoid flaunting your wealth. Use in-room safes at all times.

5. **Hotel Hack: Block Out Light with This Simple Coat Hanger Trick.** If hotel blackout curtains don't close completely, there's an easy fix: take a coat hanger with clips, turn it vertically, and use it to pinch the curtains together. This creates a tight seal to keep out any bright lights and helps ensure a restful night's sleep.

6. **Hotel Room Safety**. Request a hotel room above the first floor if traveling alone for added safety. Always lock the deadbolt and secure sliding glass doors and windows.

7. **Leave Appropriate Gratuities**. Ensure you provide suitable tips for service staff as per local customs.

8. **Maid Service**. Leave the request on your door when you are inside the room to avoid advertising your absence.

9. **Mirror Effect**. Demonstrate politeness and consideration, as this encourages others to reciprocate with similar good behavior.

10. **Protect Your Belongings**. Wear a money pouch around your neck, waist, or leg for both domestic and international travel to safeguard your valuables.

11. **Respect Hotel Property**. Do not take items from your hotel room; these are not complimentary souvenirs.

12. **Respect Local Customs**. Observe local rules, including photo restrictions and cultural norms.

13. **Room Security**. Latch the security chain on your hotel room door and always lock the deadbolt.

14. **Room Number**. Never give out your hotel information or room number to strangers.

15. **Stay Aware**. Be aware of your surroundings at all times, especially in unfamiliar areas.

16. **Wander Safely**. Carry a safety whistle for added security and remain cautious when exploring new areas.

"Let your memory be your travel bag."

~ Alexander Solzhenitsyn ~

Chapter 6:
Returning Home: Journey's End

As our journey together concludes, it's evident that the world may have evolved, but the essence of travel endures. The journey is not merely about covering miles; it's also an inward exploration. The destinations we encounter and the experiences we gather shape our understanding of both the world and ourselves. The true reward of travel lies in the connections we create—whether with diverse cultures, unfamiliar landscapes, or fellow travelers.

As you prepare to disembark, take a moment to reflect on your personal growth and the lessons learned throughout this journey. Every experience has woven new threads into the fabric of your life, offering deeper perspectives and insights. Let your future journeys be defined not just by the places you visit, but by the respect, kindness, and courtesy you bring to each interaction.

Etiquette and good behavior are not mere accessories to travel: they are your guiding compass. Ensure that each step you take leaves a positive imprint on the world and those you encounter, helping to foster a more connected world.

Embrace future travels with anticipation and excitement, applying the principles you've learned to each new experience. Share your stories, practice your knowledge, and continue fostering connections and understanding. Your journey doesn't end here; it's a continuous path of learning and growth.

"The journey not the arrival matters."

~ T.S. Eliot ~

Epilogue:
Closing Reflections

As a 25-year authority on etiquette, I consistently emphasize The Golden Rule: treating others as you wish to be treated. My brand centers on good behavior, which serves not only as a guideline for everyday life but as a cornerstone for successful and respectful travel. Whether you're navigating the crowded streets of a foreign city or savoring the tranquility of a domestic destination, the ability to empathize and put yourself in others' shoes is essential for enriching your travel experiences.

Traveling isn't just about seeing new places; it's about interacting with the world in a manner that's respectful and mindful. Understanding the customs and practices of your destination—whether it's adhering to local dress codes, knowing gratuity norms, or following local etiquette—can significantly enhance your experience. A little effort can make a big impact, reflecting respect, fostering goodwill, and often leads to more meaningful connections.

As George A. Moore once said, "A man travels the world over in search of what he needs, and returns home to find it." This quote perfectly captures the essence of travel: it's not just about the destinations, but the understanding and growth we gain along the way. In my own journeys, I've discovered that following the Golden Rule has opened doors to unforgettable experiences and lasting relationships.

As you explore the world, remember that your manners are just as vital as your passport: they unlock opportunities, shape positive experiences, and leave lasting impressions on everyone you encounter. No matter where your travels lead, carry with you the wisdom of The Golden Rule, allowing it to guide your journey toward discovery, respect, and joy.

Lisa Mirza Grotts, The Golden Rules Gal, is a storyteller and 25-year authority on etiquette, providing online etiquette training in business and social etiquette. Grotts was the former Director of Protocol for

Mayor Willie Brown in San Francisco. Her clients include Microsoft, UC Berkeley, BlackRock, Levi Strauss, American Airlines, Cornell University, and Stanford Hospital. She has been quoted by over 100 publications, including The New York Times, Newsweek, San Francisco Chronicle, Condé Nast Traveler, The Washington Post, The Wall Street Journal, Forbes, and Dear Abby. You can follow her @GoldenRulesGal on Instagram and TikTok to read her tips and stories to help you navigate the world with grace.